SPENDING PLAN SOLUTIONS

Spending Plan/Budgeting
Major Purchases-Houses and Cars

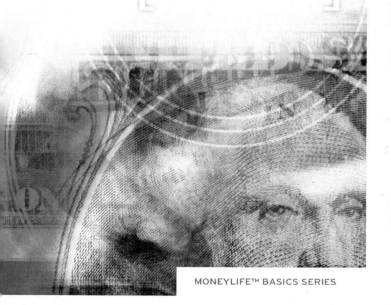

MONEYLIFE™ BASICS SERIES

ISBN 978-1-56427-252-2

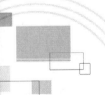

CONTENTS

INTRODUCTION

Stuck?

> It happens all the time. Somewhere, right now, someone
> is getting stuck. Sometimes people don't see the flooded
> dip in the road as they approach it. Sometimes they see
> it and think it's not deep enough to stop them. Or that if it
> does, they can just float for a bit while it goes down.

Some manage to plow through it and assume they can do the same
with the next one. Others get hung up and need to be bailed out
before resuming their journey. Still others hydroplane off the road or
into the path of oncoming traffic. Some barely escape with their lives.
Some don't.

You know we're not really talking about flash floods and cars, right?
Mismanaged finances and their accompanying stress can be just as
dangerous as a flash flood.

We don't want to be melodramatic; we just want to underscore the
point. How we handle money has serious implications. Most of us
need solutions, a plan that is better than our present habits.

Help and Hope Are Here.

*Crown exists to provide help, hope, and
insight.* These Help and Hope buttons appear
whenever special information is available to
assist and encourage you.

Whether you need a basic spending plan that will enable you to maximize the effectiveness of every dollar you earn or a strategy for dealing with big-ticket items, the solutions you need are near at hand. In fact, they are in your hands right now. You're holding them in this book. They work. Every time.

In addition to developing a plan that puts you firmly in control of your spending and allows you to deal with major purchases, some of you will want to go deeper. You'd like to see a long-term plan that lays out everything from where you are now to your goal of becoming financially faithful. CrownMoneyMap.org is a great online community that contains tools and resources to get you there, and membership is free.

Also, keep in mind that this *MoneyLife™ Basics Series* is designed to be first aid. Those needing more intensive treatment can go on to additional resources available at Crown.org. But for now:

- Do you have consumer debt? The plan will eliminate it.

- Are you giving regularly? The plan will make it a priority.

- Are you saving for retirement? The plan will put you on auto-save.

- Are you likely to need a bigger house or a different car—something that costs a lot more than the cash in your pocket? The plan will enable you to take it in stride.

Let's put the plan to work. You can do it!

Please notice a few helpful features we include in every *MoneyLife™ Basics Series* book.

1. Appendix 1 is an introduction to Christ. If you (or someone you know) are uncertain about where you stand with God, this short introduction will guide you into an intimate relationship with Him.

2. Appendix 2, "God's Ownership & Financial Faithfulness," briefly explores a fundamental concept—one that frames the correct perspective on every financial principle in Scripture. If you don't understand this, you are likely to manage your resources with worldly wisdom. The world's approach to money management isn't always evil, but it is short-sighted (ignoring eternity), incomplete (ignoring the Creator/Controller/Provider), and usually in pursuit of the wrong goals.

3. Because we are committed to transformation rather than mere information, each chapter ends with a two-part exercise:

   • An Action Step you create based on your response to the chapter

   • A Celebration Plan for every Action Step completed

Please take advantage of these to maximize your experience in this small book. James 1:22 sums it up when it says, *"Do not merely listen to the word, and so deceive yourselves. Do what it says"* (NIV).

CHAPTER 1

SPENDING PLAN/ BUDGETING

Comprehensive help for putting it all together

It seems to be a natural law of economics: Regardless of how much our income increases, our expenses manage to consume it. And then some.

Our checking accounts often resemble the formula for water; instead of two parts hydrogen for one part oxygen, substitute two parts expenses for one part income. The solution, of course, is to create a spending plan and live by it.

Many people just shoot from the hip, hoping everything will turn out okay, because taking time to track the numbers doesn't seem very enjoyable at first. Many of us don't particularly enjoy brushing our teeth, either, but we've learned that the discipline beats the alternative—by a long shot.

> **Bad news:** Creating a spending plan will take some time and effort.
>
> **Good news:** It will be customized to meet your needs.
>
> **Better news:** It will save lots of time and effort in years to come.
>
> **Best news:** It will pay off for the rest of your life.

Rather than being an inflexible straitjacket, a spending plan delivers surprising freedom. It removes mystery, fear and the exhaustion of struggling to keep our noses above the water line of debt.

Steps to Create a Spending Plan

Creating a spending plan that fits you perfectly is the goal for this chapter. We'll follow several logical steps in the process. We'll also provide helpful forms in two versions, one with with sample numbers plugged in for illustration and one with blanks to fill in.

Step 1—List Monthly Household Expenditures.

a. Fixed Expenses

- Tithe
- Federal income taxes (if taxes are deducted, ignore this item)
- State income taxes (if taxes are deducted, ignore this item)
- Federal Social Security taxes (if taxes are deducted, ignore this item)
    - Housing expenses (payment/rent)
        - Residence (Real Estate) taxes
            - Residence insurance
                - Other

b. Variable Expenses

- Food
- Outstanding debts
- Utilities
- Insurance (life, health, auto)
- Entertainment/recreation
- Clothing allowance
- Medical/dental
- Savings/miscellaneous

NOTE: In order to accurately determine variable expenses, both husband and wife should keep an expense diary for 30 days. Every expenditure, even small purchases, should be listed.

Step 2—List Available Monthly Income.

NOTE: If your income varies from month to month, use a yearly average divided by 12 to establish a monthly average.

- Salary
- Rents
- Interest
- Dividends
- Income tax refund
- Notes (loans you have made to others that they are repaying you)
- Other

Step 3—Compare Income Versus Expenses.

We encourage couples to base their spending plan, as much as possible, on one spouse's income—thereby reducing the family's vulnerability to lost income due to illness, pregnancy, or a change in employment location. The other spouse's income can be allocated to one-time purchases—vacations, furniture, cars—or to savings, debt reduction or giving.

If you are in the fortunate position of having total income that exceeds total expenses, your spending plan's primary role will be to speed your progress towards the ultimate goal of financial faithfulness—including the ability to serve in any way God directs without the need of a salary.

If, however, your expenses exceed income (or you simply desire more stringent controls in spending), you will need to analyze each spending plan category to reduce expenses. These categories are outlined below along with some guidance for the percentage of your income they will probably require.

"Budget busters" are the large potential problem areas that routinely ruin a spending plan. Failure to control even one of these problems can result in a family financial disaster.

The percentage of net income we suggest for each category is based on successful spending plans for families of four with a $45,000 annual income. These percentages are not absolutes and will vary with income and geographic location.

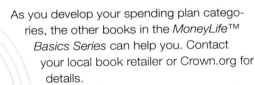

As you develop your spending plan categories, the other books in the *MoneyLife*™ *Basics Series* can help you. Contact your local book retailer or Crown.org for details.

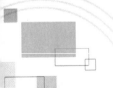

a. Housing (32 percent of net income)

Typically, this is one of the largest spending plan problems. Many families buy homes they can't afford. The decision to buy or rent should be based on needs and financial ability rather than on peer pressure or an unrealistic expectation of gain.

b. Food (13 percent of net income)

Many families buy too much food. Others buy too little. The average American family tends to buy the wrong type of food. The reduction of a family's food bill requires quantity and quality planning.

Hints for Grocery Shopping

- Always use a written list of needs.

- Try to conserve gas by buying food for a longer time period and in larger quantities.

- Avoid buying when hungry.

- Use a calculator, if possible, to keep a running subtotal.

- Reduce or eliminate paper products—paper plates, cups, napkins (use cloth napkins).

- Evaluate where to purchase sundry items, such as shampoo, mouthwash. (These are usually less expensive at discount stores.)

- Avoid processed and sugar-coated cereals. (These are expensive and most of them have little nutritional value.)

- Avoid prepared foods, such as frozen dinners, pot pies, cakes. (You are paying for expensive labor that you can provide.)

- Determine good meat cuts that are available from roasts or shoulders, and have the butcher cut these for you. (Buying steaks by the package on sale is fairly inexpensive also.)

- Try store brand canned products. (These are normally cheaper and just as nutritious.)

- Avoid products in a seasonal price hike. Substitute or eliminate.

- Shop for advertised specials. (These are usually posted in the store window.)

- Use manufacturer's coupons (cents-off on an item or items) only if you were going to buy the item anyway and it is cheaper than another brand without the coupon.

- When possible, purchase food in bulk quantities from large discount stores; the per-item cost is cheaper. Do not buy from convenience stores except in case of emergency.

- Avoid buying non-grocery items in a grocery supermarket except on sale. (These are normally "high mark-up" items.)

  - For baby foods, use normal foods processed in a blender.

    - If possible, leave children at home with a responsible adult to avoid unnecessary pressure.

- Check every item as it is being "rung up" at the store and again when you get home.

- Consider canning fresh vegetables whenever possible. Make bulk purchases with other families at farmers' markets or wherever you can get the best value. (NOTE: Buy canning supplies during off seasons.)

c. Transportation (13 percent of net income)

The advertising media refers to us as "consumers," but that's not always the best description. P.T. Barnum had a more apt word—"suckers." Often we are unwise in our decision making when it comes to machines—especially cars.

Many families will buy new cars they cannot afford and trade them much sooner than necessary. Those who buy a new car, keeping it for less than four years and then trading it for another new car, waste the maximum amount of money. Some people, such as salespeople who drive a great deal, need new cars frequently; most of us do not. We swap cars because we want to—not because we have to.

d. Insurance (5 percent of net income)

Few people understand insurance, resulting in poor decisions and lost money. Some buy high-cost insurance they don't need and can't afford; others have none, exposing themselves to unacceptable risk. It is important to know what kind and how much is needed.

Insurance should be used as supplementary provision for the family, not for profit. An insurance plan is not designed for saving money or for retirement. Ask anyone who assumed it was; the ultimate result was disillusionment.

One of your best insurance assets is to have a trustworthy agent who will create a simple plan to analyze your exact needs. Independent agents can select from several different companies to provide you with the best possible options.

e. Debts (5 percent of net income)

It would be great if most budgets included 5 percent debts or less. Unfortunately, the norm in American families is far in excess of this amount because of the proliferation of credit cards, bank loans, and installment credit. What can you do once this situation exists?

- Destroy all credit cards as a first step.

- Establish a payment schedule that includes all creditors.

- Contact all creditors, honestly relate your problems, and arrange an equitable repayment plan.

- Buy on a cash basis, and sacrifice your wants and desires until you are current.

f. Entertainment/Recreation (5 percent of net income)

We are a recreation-oriented culture. That is not necessarily bad if put in the proper perspective. But those who are in debt cannot use their creditor's money to entertain themselves. The normal tendency is to escape pain for the moment—even if the problems then become more acute. We must resist this urge and control recreation and entertainment expenses while in debt.

What a terrible witness it is for a follower of Christ who is in financial bondage to indulge at the expense of others. God knows we need rest and relaxation; once our attitude is correct, He will often provide it from unexpected sources. Every believer, whether in debt or not, should seek to reduce entertainment expenses. This usually can be done without sacrificing quality family time.

Recreation Hints

- Plan vacations during "off seasons" if possible.

- Consider a camping vacation to avoid motel and food expenses. (Christian friends can pool the expenses of camping items.)

- Select vacation areas in your general locale.

- Use some family games in place of movies (like some of those unused games received at Christmas).

- To reduce expenses and increase fellowship, consider taking vacation trips with two or more families.

- If flying, use the least expensive coach fare. Flexibility in day of the week or even time of day can result in significant savings.

g. Clothing (5 percent of net income)

Many families in debt sacrifice this area in their budget because of excesses in other areas. Prudent planning and buying can clothe any family neatly without great expense.

- Save enough money to buy without using credit.

- Educate family members on care of clothing.

- Apply discipline with children to enforce these habits.

- Develop skills in making and mending clothing.

- Avoid the trap of fashion/fad consciousness—especially when it means buying expensive labels for no functional reason. When possible, buy clothes with a classic style that meet a need rather than clothes that make a temporary fashion statement.

Budget Hints

- Make a written list of clothing needs and purchase during the "off" season when possible.

- Select outfits that can be mixed and used in multiple combinations rather than as a single set.

- Shop the discount outlets that carry unmarked name-brand goods.

- Shop at authentic factory outlet stores for close-out values of top quality.

- Watch garage sales, consignment shops and Goodwill-type stores for outstanding values.

- Select clothing made of home-washable fabrics.

  - Use coin-operated dry cleaning machines instead of commercial cleaners.

    - Practice early repair for damaged clothing.

      - Learn to utilize all clothing fully (especially children's wear).

h. Savings (5 percent of net income)

It is important to establish regular saving in your spending plan. Without a habit of saving, the use of credit and its resulting debt becomes a lifelong prison.

Savings Hints

- Use a company payroll withdrawal, if possible. This removes the money before you receive it.

- Use an automatic bank withdrawal from your checking account into your savings account.

- Write a check to your savings account just as if it were a creditor.

- Begin saving at least a small monthly amount now. When you have paid off all consumer debts, allocate those monthly amounts to savings.

i. Medical/dental expenses (6 percent of net income)

You must anticipate these expenses in your budget and set aside funds regularly; failure to do so will wreck your plans and lead to indebtedness. Do not sacrifice family health due to lack of planning; but, at the same time, do not use doctors excessively. Proper prevention is much cheaper than correction.

You can avoid many dental bills by teaching children to eat the right foods and to clean their teeth properly. Your dentist will supply all the information you need on this subject.

Many doctor bills can be avoided in the same way. Taking proper care of your body through diet, rest and exercise will usually reward you with good health. Abusing your body may not result in immediate consequences, but you will ultimately pay through illnesses and malfunctions. This is not to say that all illnesses or problems are caused by neglect, but a great many are.

Don't hesitate to question doctors and dentists in advance about costs. Also, educate yourself enough to discern when you are getting good value for your money. Most ethical professionals will not take offense at your questions. If they do, it may be a hint to change providers.

Shop around for prescriptions. You will be amazed at the wide variance in prices from one store to the next. Ask about generic drugs. These are usually much less expensive and are just as effective.

j. Miscellaneous and variable expenses (6 percent of net income)

Some of these expenses occur monthly, and others occur on an as-needed basis (such as appliances).

One of the most important factors in home expenses is you. If you can perform routine maintenance and repair, considerable expenses can be avoided. If, on the other hand, you are just handy enough to turn a $50 repair into a $200 mess, you'll need to decide whether you have the aptitude for a particular job. Still, routine maintenance is usually more of an "elbow grease" issue.

Many people rationalize not doing these things on the basis that their time is too valuable. Although this argument may have some merit for people who earn much more per hour than a repairman costs, unless they can earn it for as many hours as they want any time they want, it is probably a weak argument. And even for those who can earn around the clock, every hour of the day should not be tied up in the pursuit of money.

A part of care and maintenance around the home relates to family life, particularly the training of children. When they see Mom and Dad willing to do some physical labor to help around the home, they will learn good habits. But if you refuse to get involved, why should they? Where will they ever learn the skills of self-sufficiency?

Some men avoid working on home projects because they say they lack the necessary skills. Well, those skills are learned, not gifted. There are many good books, often found in your local library, that detail every area of home maintenance. At some point in the future, many of these skills are likely to be necessities rather than choices.

k. Investments (5 percent of net income)

Individuals and families with surplus income in their budgets will have the opportunity to invest for retirement or other long-term goals. This recommended percentage is a great starting amount, and then as debt-free status is achieved, more money can be diverted to this category.

l. School/Child care (5 percent of net income)
(If this category is used, other categories must be adjusted downward a total of 5 percent.)

A growing number of families choose private school and/ or child care for their children. This category is for those expenses. Because this is an elective, it is not included within the normal 100 percent allotment, so other categories must be reduced to provide these funds.

m. Unallocated Surplus Income

Income from unallocated sources (garage sales, gifts) can be kept in the checking account and placed in this category. This category is also useful for recording income information for tax purposes.

Variable Income Planning

Families with variable monthly incomes need a spending plan even more than families on fixed salaries. Many people with fluctuating incomes get trapped into debt because they spend what they make during high-income months and borrow during lean months rather than anticipating and saving for them.

Living on a fluctuating income can be very deceiving—and difficult. Months of high income can easily be construed as the new norm or a windfall profit to be spent on non-necessities. To properly manage variable income, conservatively estimate what your annual income is likely to be. Divide it by 12, and then use that amount as the monthly income for your plan. Put all your income into a savings account and withdraw your plan amount each month.

This method will allow surplus funds from higher-income months to accumulate in the savings account to provide the normal planned income during months of

actual lower income. This is not hoarding;
it is planning according to Proverbs 6:6-8.

Pulling It All Together

Now that you have seen the general categories of
expenses, one thing should be clear. Creating a spending plan
is not mysterious magic. Nor is it too complicated. Although
some people make a hobby of it and use sophisticated
software that can generate a hundred different reports to give
alternate views of the same information, others get by just fine
with a fistful of hand-labeled envelopes.

The basic steps are simple.

1. Track all of your expenses for a month. Everything. (Include a monthly estimate for expenses you pay every three months or six months, etc.)

2. List your income for the month.

3. Compare the totals to determine whether you are spending more than you earn.

4. List your expenses in the category where they belong.

5. Check to see whether your category totals are within the suggested percentage of income.

6. Make any necessary adjustments (either to income or spending or both) to create a monthly surplus.

7. Spend according to plan, using discipline and patience to avoid violating your plan.

Remember that the race to accumulate usually ends at a different finish line than we expect. Effective advertising promises a finish line of wealth and happiness. Reality delivers a finish line of high stress, a crater of debt, and often the loss of the very things we worked so hard to get. Don't be the rabbit, getting caught up in the race.

Instead, be the tortoise, content to make slow, steady progress toward your goals. This is not hard; it's just countercultural. And it's God's way. *"The plans of the diligent lead to profit as surely as haste leads to poverty"* (Proverbs 21:5, NIV). The Contemporary English Version says it this way: *"If you plan and work hard, you will have plenty; if you get in a hurry, you will end up poor."*

Bottom line? You can do this. The forms at the end of the chapter will guide you. Go to CrownMoneyMap.org for additional help. A free online journey to developing financial faithfulness awaits you.

A Journey of Faith:
Glenn and Susan Preston

God, the Creator and Owner of all things, has promised to provide for our needs. We show our gratitude when we are accountable to Him through a budget that helps us spend wisely.

Glenn and Susan Preston of Oakwood, Georgia, can attest to the reality of that promise. They are the parents of six children ranging in ages from 2 to 16 years, but only Glenn works full time.

First exposure to Crown

Early in his life, Glenn was introduced to the teachings of Larry Burkett by a co-worker, Vicky Putman, and her husband Dennis.

"Dennis had listened to Larry's tapes in the mid-1980s and decided he wanted Vicky to stay home with the kids," Glenn says. "So he became his family's sole provider. He gave me a stack of Larry's tapes and explained the importance of living on a budget. He was living by those principles himself."

Unfortunately, Glenn wasn't completely ready to put Dennis' advice into practice. Not long after this, he married his wife Susan, and early in their marriage they had financial problems.

The couple moved to Auburn, Alabama, where he was going to attend graduate school and she planned to work full time. But six months after the wedding, Susan learned she was pregnant and chose to stay home with their child.

Glenn earned money through a teaching assistantship while attending graduate school to study physical education. He also worked from 3 p.m. to 11 p.m. on Saturdays and Sundays at a local hospital.

"It wasn't the smartest way to do things," he says. "I should have gotten a full-time job and gone to school part time."

However, God provided for the couple through a number of means, including help from their parents.

Crown for the second time

Glenn's physical education career eventually took him to North Georgia College and State University in Dahlonega, Georgia, where Don Delozier, an instructor for Crown, presented a seminar at his church.

Once again, Glenn was shown the need to handle his money according to God's financial principles.

He and Susan had a large amount of credit card debt, so he sought Don's help in developing a budget. "Don told us to be faithful and watch God bless," Glenn says, noting that he and Susan received an unexpected windfall that allowed them to completely repay their debts.

However, when Glenn moved into his current job as fitness center director and facilities coordinator at Gainesville College, he lost touch with his budget. He and Susan moved to Oakwood, Georgia, where the college is located, and their expenses changed. "I didn't update our budget," he says, "and our debt started mounting."

A third encounter with Crown

Recently, Glenn went through Crown's life group study, which takes participants through a deep journey into God's Word.

"I had done the mechanical part," he says, "but the Scriptures made the difference. This time I got a heart transplant. I had never seen that the way you handle money affects your intimacy with Christ. Every day you're in the study, you're in the Scriptures, and the Scriptures will change your heart."

One portion of the study that impressed Susan was the chapter on work. She has since started a small home business selling gourmet foods, which gives her an occasional break and fellowship with other women. Susan is also teaching biblical financial principles to middle school girls at her church.

In late January, Glenn and Susan had the opportunity to tell people across the nation about the manner in which God has changed their finances. During a CBS television special about the growing national interest in the Bible's view on money, Crown Financial Ministries was featured. A CBS camera crew set up their equipment in the couple's home and allowed them to share their story.

"For Susan and me, Crown has been life-changing," Glenn says. "We appreciate the time and effort put into the re-sources Crown provides. We're grateful to Crown's cofounder Howard Dayton and to his business partner, Jim Seneff, for the effort they made to search the Scriptures and to discover all that God has to say about managing our money." ■

Your Response

So what do I do now?

On the next page, we encourage you to write at least one Ac-tion Step in response to the chapter you have just read. If you write more than one, prioritize them in a logical order so you have a clear first step that you can begin immediately.

Action Steps _____

_____

_____

_____

_____

_____

We also encourage you to reward yourself for every Action Step completed. Since the enemy ("the accuser") will discourage you by making the journey seem impossibly long, you need to see each step as its own victory. Your progress will be faster and more enjoyable if you take a little time to celebrate it.

Your celebration doesn't have to take a lot of time or money to be meaningful. Just make it something you enjoy, and tie it to the Action Step you have completed.

Celebration Plan _____

_____

_____

_____

_____

_____

_____

Estimated Spending Plan

Date _____

MONTHLY INCOME

GROSS MONTHLY INCOME		**$3,790**
Salary	3,750	
Interest	5	
Dividends	15	
Other Income	20	
Less		
1. **Tithe/Giving**		379
2. **Taxes** (Federal, State, FICA)		750
NET SPENDABLE INCOME		**$2,661**

MONTHLY LIVING EXPENSES

3. **Housing**		**$853**
Mortgage/Rent	650	
Insurance	20	
Property taxes	50	
Cable TV	0	
Electricity	60	
Gas	12	
Water	10	
Sanitation	0	
Telephone	25	
Maintenance	26	
Internet service	0	
Other	0	
4. **Food**		373
5. **Transportation**		345
Payments	100	
Gas & Oil	75	
Insurance	50	
License/Taxes	40	
Maintenance	50	
Replacement	30	
Other	0	
6. **Insurance**		105
Life	40	
Health/Dental	65	
Disability	0	

Other	0	
7. **Debts** (not including house or auto)		133
8. **Entertainment/Recreation**		133
Eating out	83	
Babysitters	0	
Activities/Trips	20	
Vacation	30	
Pets	0	
Other	0	
9. **Clothing**		133
10. **Savings**		133
11. **Medical/Dental**		160
Doctor	60	
Dentist	50	
Prescriptions	50	
Other	0	
12. **Miscellaneous**		160
Toiletries/Cosmetics	19	
Beauty/Barber	20	
Laundry/Cleaners	15	
Allowances	45	
Subscriptions	15	
Gifts	46	
Other	0	
13. **Investments**		133
14. **School/Child Care**		0
Tuition	0	
Materials	0	
Transportation	0	
Day care	0	
TOTAL LIVING EXPENSES		**$2,661**

HOW THE MONTH TURNS OUT

NET SPENDABLE INCOME	**$2,661**
- TOTAL LIVING EXPENSES	**$2,661**
= SURPLUS OR DEFICIT	**0**

Estimated Spending Plan

Date _____

MONTHLY INCOME

GROSS MONTHLY INCOME _____

    Salary _____
    Interest _____
    Dividends _____
    Other Income _____

Less

1. **Tithe/Giving** _____
2. **Taxes** (Federal, State, FICA) _____

NET SPENDABLE INCOME _____

MONTHLY LIVING EXPENSES

3. **Housing** _____
    Mortgage/Rent _____
    Insurance _____
    Property taxes _____
    Cable TV _____
    Electricity _____
    Gas _____
    Water _____
    Sanitation _____
    Telephone _____
    Maintenance _____
    Internet service _____
    Other _____

4. **Food** _____

5. **Transportation** _____
    Payments _____
    Gas & Oil _____
    Insurance _____
    License/Taxes _____
    Maintenance _____
    Replacement _____
    Other _____

6. **Insurance** _____
    Life _____
    Health/Dental _____
    Disability _____

    Other _____

7. **Debts** (not including house or auto) _____

8. **Entertainment/Recreation** _____
    Eating out _____
    Babysitters _____
    Activities/Trips _____
    Vacation _____
    Pets _____
    Other _____

9. **Clothing** _____

10. **Savings** _____

11. **Medical/Dental** _____
    Doctor _____
    Dentist _____
    Prescriptions _____
    Other _____

12. **Miscellaneous** _____
    Toiletries/Cosmetics _____
    Beauty/Barber _____
    Laundry/Cleaners _____
    Allowances _____
    Subscriptions _____
    Gifts _____
    Other _____

13. **Investments** _____

14. **School/Child Care** _____
    Tuition _____
    Materials _____
    Transportation _____
    Day care _____

TOTAL LIVING EXPENSES _____

HOW THE MONTH TURNS OUT

NET SPENDABLE INCOME _____

- TOTAL LIVING EXPENSES _____

= SURPLUS OR DEFICIT _____

Percentage Spending Plan

Date _____   **SAMPLE**

Annual Income: $ 45,480

Gross Income		$ 3,790
1. Tithe/Giving		$ 379
2. Taxes		$ 750
Net Spendable Income		$ 2,661

Spending Category	Percentage		NSI*		Amount
3. Housing	32%	X	2,661	= $	853
4. Food	13%	X	2,661	= $	345
5. Transportation	13%	X	2,661	= $	345
6. Insurance	5%	X	2,661	= $	133
7. Debts	5%	X	2,661	= $	133
8. Entertainment/Recreation	5%	X	2,661	= $	133
9. Clothing	5%	X	2,661	= $	133
10. Savings	5%	X	2,661	= $	133
11. Medical/Dental	6%	X	2,661	= $	160
12. Miscellaneous	6%	X	2,661	= $	160
13. Investments	5%	X	2,661	= $	133
14. School/Child Care[1]	0%	X	0	= $	0
Total (cannot exceed Net Spendable Income)				$	2,661

*Net Spendable Income

[1] If you have this expense, this percentage must be deducted from other spending plan categories.

Percentage Spending Plan

Date _____

Annual Income: $_____

Gross Income	$_____
1. Tithe/Giving	$_____
2. Taxes	$_____
Net Spendable Income	$_____

Spending Category	Percentage		NSI*		Amount
3. Housing	_____	X	_____	=	$_____
4. Food	_____	X	_____	=	$_____
5. Transportation	_____	X	_____	=	$_____
6. Insurance	_____	X	_____	=	$_____
7. Debts	_____	X	_____	=	$_____
8. Entertainment/Recreation	_____	X	_____	=	$_____
9. Clothing	_____	X	_____	=	$_____
10. Savings	_____	X	_____	=	$_____
11. Medical/Dental	_____	X	_____	=	$_____
12. Miscellaneous	_____	X	_____	=	$_____
13. Investments	_____	X	_____	=	$_____
14. School/Child Care[1]	_____	X	_____	=	$_____
Total (cannot exceed Net Spendable Income)					$_____

*Net Spendable Income

[1] If you have this expense, this percentage must be deducted from other spending plan categories.

2 MAJOR PURCHASES

Buying Houses and Cars

Major purchases are inevitable. Most people expect to buy a house or a car at some point. Even a new refrigerator at $1,000 to $2,000 can be a challenge.

Although it is possible for any expense category to get out of line and ruin a spending plan, nothing will do it quicker than a major purchase. But it doesn't have to be that way.

Think of major purchases as wild mustangs invading your fenced corral. They threaten to scatter your horses, leaving you with nothing. You could build a higher, stronger fence and keep them out, but you would rather have the benefits they offer. What if you could tame them enough to allow them into the corral and keep them there?

This is what we are about to do. Careful planning can tame the major purchases that threaten to destroy our finances by causing us to spend more than we earn. With wise planning and applying biblical wisdom, you can successfully make major purchases and develop a lifestyle of financial faithfulness at the same time.

Housing

Let's talk first about the cost of housing. Since it is the greatest expense most of us ever incur, we should carefully consider several complex variables before making a commitment. And because we are in management of God's possessions, our first responsibility is to pray for His guidance regarding all financial decisions.

Carefully research the housing market along with available financing. Your personal situation—including your spending plan, which is detailed in Chapter 1—also sheds light on whether buying or renting is best at any given time.

Your spending plan lets you know how much is coming in, how much is going out, and areas in which you can cut costs. This allows you to take the monthly amount you would be required to pay on a certain house and see whether it will fit.

Buying a house without first making sure it fits your spending plan can place a tremendous financial burden on your family. Limiting yourself to a house within your spending plan may require you to settle for a smaller house than you desire, but one thing is for sure: The less you owe on your house, the sooner you can pay it off.

Then, you can take the money you were using to make payments and invest it for your children's college or for retirement. The state of our nation's economy is another reason to pay off your house early. The continuous buildup of federal debt must eventually produce severe economic consequences—especially for individuals with heavy debt burdens.

Having a written spending plan and living within it is the first step in buying a house. Although your financial situation will be the major factor in determining what type of housing you need, there are other factors to consider. Prayerfully give these questions some thought.

1. Is your job secure enough for you to make mortgage payments? If not, consider renting instead of buying.

2. How long do you plan to stay in the area? If you know you will be staying in the community for at least five years, house ownership may be a good option.

3. What is the economy like in the area you are considering? Is the area growing substantially? Will the house appreciate? You don't want to be stuck with a house that is hard to sell because of the local economy.

4. What is the cost of living in the new area? If it is high, it will definitely affect your budget and may change the amount you can afford for housing.

After answering these questions, take the amount you can spend for housing and determine if house payments, including taxes, insurance, maintenance, and utilities would be equal to or less than rental payments for a similar house in the same area. If they are, then buying a house may be a wise choice.

Biblical Principles Regarding Debt

Since we've already covered this subject in *Debt and Bankruptcy*, the first book of the *MoneyLife™ Basics Series*, we'll limit this discussion to a few reminders.

1. The Bible doesn't prohibit borrowing, but it does discourage it. In fact, every biblical reference to borrowing is a negative one.

2. Borrowing is literally a vow to repay, and God requires us to keep our vows.

3. Surety means taking on an obligation to pay without a guaranteed way to pay it.

Until the 1980s, many banks did not require a personal guarantee (surety) for a home loan. They allowed the home to stand as sole collateral. In today's economy, however, with higher costs and lower down payments, the rules have changed.

Since most homeowners can no longer avoid surety, we recommend that you:

1. buy a home well within your means,

2. make a large enough down payment to reduce the potential risk,

3. and pay off the mortgage as quickly as possible.

With wisdom-filled planning, your home purchase can be more fun, exciting, and peaceful than you ever imagined!

Housing Options

If you've decided that buying a house fits into your spending plan and is in your best long-term interest, you can begin to look at the options available to you.

Included in these options are new and used houses, condominiums, and mobile homes.

New House Pros ☺ and Cons ☹

☺ You can design it to fit your individual needs.

☹ It will probably cost much more than you think after paying for changes and upgrades, hidden expenses, window treatments, landscaping, etc.

☹ Overseeing the construction of a new house requires many decisions and takes considerable time and effort.

Used House Pros ☺ and Cons ☹

☺ You know exactly what the house will cost.

☺ It will likely come with many extras included: curtains, curtain rods, towel racks, ceiling fans, lights in the closets, light bulbs, an established lawn, shrubbery, and occasionally even appliances. Be sure the contract states exactly which items will come with the house.

☹ The condition may show wear and tear, which means repairs. The older the house is, the more repairs it's likely to need. Always check the heating and air conditioning, roof, water heater, and appliances to see if they are in working condition. You may choose to hire a house inspection service to do this for you. (Look under Building Inspection or Inspection Bureaus in the Yellow Pages.) After the house has been checked, you can decide whether to purchase the house as is or back out of the deal.

The Fixer-Upper or Handyman's Special

Fixer-uppers usually sell for well below normal market price. Some of this is due to their lack of visual appeal. If you can look past this, you may have a diamond in the rough. Keep in mind, though, that some of the lower price will be lost through above-average repair costs.

Be sure to have the house checked thoroughly, including foundations, roof, plumbing, and wiring, so you know exactly what is wrong with the house before you buy it. If you have the skills and don't mind doing the repairs, you can make a nice profit when you sell it.

Condominiums

Make sure you know all additional costs, such as maintenance fees and club fees, and have them factored into your spending plan.

Be aware that the maintenance fees are subject to change each year, and you have no control over them. This is not a bad option, especially if you don't want to bother with yard work.

Mobile Homes

Although some people won't consider living in manufactured housing, others think they are a great value.

As with a car, a new mobile home may lose about 25 percent of its total value when it leaves the sales lot. Consider buying a previously owned mobile home, because someone else has already taken the depreciation.

Financing

Now that you've decided what type of house you want to buy, you need to decide how to pay for it.

Pay Cash

The best way to buy a house is to pay cash. Our modern culture wants too much too fast, making this approach the rare exception. A good compromise, however, is to

- buy a smaller house,
- invest time and effort into improving its value,
- sell it, and
- buy the next larger size house.

This approach rewards the patient with their dream house and little or no debt.

Institutional Loans

These loans, issued by banks, savings and loans, credit unions, and mortgage companies, are the most common type of financing for a house purchase. It's important to shop around, because there are so many variables in the rates and terms.

Fees and Contracts

Most institutional loans require a down payment, usually between 5 and 20 percent. But remember, the more you put down, the less likely you are to have a problem with surety.

In addition, there are various closing costs.

- Loan origination fees
- Points
- Attorneys' fees
- Survey fees
- Inspection fees
- Appraisal fees
- PMI (private mortgage insurance)
- Real estate commissions
- Credit reports
- Title search fees

These fees can add up to quite an expense—several thousand dollars—and should be researched thoroughly when considering any loan. Many times the seller may pay for some or all of the closing costs.

If your offer to purchase the house is subject to selling your present house, getting financial approval, or waiting on results from various inspections, be sure these contingencies are included in the contract.

You would be wise to have the property tested for any conditions that might apply, including radon gas, termites, structural defects, water problems, and non-working appliances.

Fixed-rate Mortgages

The fixed-rate mortgage is an excellent house loan. You know exactly what the interest rate and monthly mortgage payment will be and whether it will fit into your budget.

Although a fixed-rate loan will have a slightly higher interest rate than adjustable-rate loans, it is well worth the additional cost if you anticipate keeping the loan for several years. You have the benefit of knowing that your monthly principal and interest payment will not change during the life of the loan.

The shorter the mortgage, the less interest you will pay. A 15-year mortgage usually has three advantages over a 30-year:

1. You cut your risk in half by owning your home free and clear in half the time.

2. You pay much less interest because of the shorter time.

3. You can usually get a better interest rate (by a half-percent) for a 15-year.

Nevertheless, many people are better off to get a 30-year mortgage and treat it as a 15-year. By making larger payments than the required minimum, they can reduce the term to 15 years or even less, achieving the first two advantages shown above. But if they encounter a difficult financial stretch, they are not required to make a payment as large as the 15-year mortgage would demand.

Since rates vary from institution to institution and from week to week, shop around for the best rates and terms.

Adjustable Rate Mortgages (ARMs)

ARMs are not a bad option under certain conditions. If you can answer "yes" to these three questions, an ARM might be attractive for your situation.

1. Do you plan to sell the house or refinance the loan within two to three years?

2. Will your initial rate be at least 1 to 2 percent lower than the fixed rate?

3. Does the loan put caps on the maximum annual interest-rate increase as well as the absolute maximum during the life of the loan?

Since these loans fluctuate with the economy, it's crucial to know exactly how high the interest rate could go.

Most ARMs begin with an interest rate that's a percentage point or two below current fixed-rate loans; then they periodically adjust after that. This allows more people to qualify for them, but it also makes it harder to determine how much to allocate for housing from year to year in your spending plan.

Be sure you understand the terms before you choose an ARM. For example, if you get a 7 percent ARM with a 5 percent cap, your rate could climb to 12 percent. Let's suppose the current fixed rate is 9 percent. If the terms of the adjustable are such that you could go above the fixed rate of 9 percent after just two or three years, then you probably are better off taking the fixed rate.

You also need to consider whether your budget can make the payments if the ARM goes up to the maximum.

Payday or Bi-monthly Mortgages

These mortgages are designed to increase the frequency of your loan payments. Instead of paying a monthly payment, you pay one-half the monthly pay-

ment every other week or one-quarter of the payment every week. This type of mortgage payment results in one extra payment per year.

Since part of the payment is applied to the principal earlier and an extra payment is made each year, equity accrues at a faster rate. You pay off the loan sooner and save interest. Most lenders who offer this option make an additional charge for it, partially offsetting the advantage. You can avoid these charges completely by staying with an ordinary mortgage and simply paying a little more than required every month.

Assumable Mortgages

These mortgages rarely exist anymore. If you find a house for sale with an assumable mortgage, the remaining amount of the mortgage will probably be low because it doesn't have many years left. Check the terms carefully before placing a lot of value on it.

Government Financing

VA, FHA, and state-bonded programs may be obtained through your local banking institution. They may have lower interest rates and lower down payments.

Seller Financing (Land Sale Contract, Trust Deed)

Some sellers will finance a house for the buyer. This provides a steady income to the seller, and the buyer usually saves on closing costs. Be sure a qualified attorney draws up all the legal papers so there is no question about the terms of the sale.

Equity Sharing

Equity sharing is an excellent way for a buyer to get help in purchasing a house. It also allows an investor to receive a healthy return on a relatively small investment. Here is how it works.

1. A buyer who needs help raising a down payment finds an investor willing to loan part of it.

2. They write an agreement that specifies a period of years that the buyer must live in the house before selling it and the amount of equity the investors receive upon sale. Although they can agree on any terms they choose, it is common for the investors to receive their initial investment back plus 50 percent of any profit.

It's possible that when the agreed-upon selling time comes, the original buyer will want to continue living there. This situation should be dealt with in advance—when the agreement is written—by including a provision that says the investor's loan will be repaid with a predetermined amount of interest. To avoid misunderstandings and strained relationships, a good Christian attorney should be involved in the preparation of any equity-sharing plan.

Parent-Assisted Financing

Many parents delight in helping their children reasonably—being careful to not take all the burdens off them. Consider this scenario. Parents provide the down payment for a son or daughter to buy a house. The house is in joint ownership: the parents own part and the children own part. The parents make the payments on the house and then rent it to the children for an amount equal to the payments. The parents depreciate the house, taking the deduction off their taxes. The children are responsible for repairing and maintaining the house, and when they eventually sell it, they receive the profit.

This method of financing benefits both parents and children. It may also be used by Christians who are willing to help other young Christian couples get their first house.

Parents with substantial savings may also choose to be lenders for their children—making the mortgage themselves. This saves money on closing costs and can provide a source of retirement income for the parents. They will need to gauge their children's maturity and make sure they are responsible enough to handle this generosity without either being spoiled or taking advantage of their parents.

Parental financing should be viewed by both parties with the same financial commitment and consequences as any other type of financing.

All legal forms should be on record so there will be no questions if the parents or the children pass away or if there is a default.

Refinance Issues

If interest rates fall after you buy your house, you'll probably be tempted to refinance. But just because rates are 1 or 2 percent lower doesn't mean you should refinance immediately.

First, determine the dollar amount of interest you would save through refinancing and compare that to the costs of new loan fees, title searches, surveys, and appraisals.

If you can easily reclaim these expenses through the savings in interest within a few years, refinancing is a good idea for you. You'll usually benefit from refinancing if the new rate is at least 3 percent lower than the rate on your present mortgage.

Whatever financing option you choose, pray earnestly for God's wisdom and give Him an opportunity to show you the best option. Trust Him to reveal each step in the process, and have an attitude of expectancy.

Real Estate Questions

What Happens If the Bank Forecloses on My House?

Although foreclosure is a serious problem, it does not mean God has washed His hands of you. As a result of losing a house, you will learn a costly but valuable lesson on the danger of surety.

When you enter into a contract, you are bound by your word to fulfill its intent. As Psalm 37:21 says, *"The wicked borrows and does not pay back, but the righteous is gracious and gives."*

Once the foreclosure has been finalized, work out a payment plan for the difference between the amount of your mortgage and the price the lender receives from the sale of the house. Be sure this payment plan will fit into your adjusted budget.

The lender will always have the option to file a deficiency judgment against you and may retain this right for several years. Check your state laws. The lender may choose to release you from the deficiency debt and has the right to do so. You must commit to pay the deficiency and do whatever the lender requests.

If you are fortunate enough to deed the house as total payment to the lender instead of going through foreclosure, you may avoid paying anything, but you will still lose the house and equity.

If you've fallen behind on your payment or must move quickly, make every effort to sell your house, even if you have to take a loss. Since foreclosed houses are generally sold at auction for much less than fair market value, the ease of letting someone else handle it will probably cost you a bundle.

What Type of Insurance Should I Have on My House?

Most lending institutions require that you have enough insurance to cover the amount of the mortgage. A homeowner's policy is a comprehensive insurance plan that covers the house, its contents, and any liability associated with the property. It is the best and least expensive way to insure a dwelling.

Costs vary significantly from one insurance company to another, so shop carefully before you buy any kind of insurance. Most insurance companies provide special insurance for condominiums and mobile homes as well.

Should I Have Life Insurance on My House?

Yes. Commonly called mortgage life insurance, it's usually sold through the lender from whom you received your house loan. But this can be a very expensive way to purchase life insurance. A decreasing term insurance policy through your local insurance agent may be less expensive.

The best approach is to determine what your total life insurance needs are and include your house loan balance with this.

By purchasing one policy, you will save money, compared to the cost of several life insurance policies. As your need for death protection diminishes, you can reduce your coverage.

Your House as an Investment

Historically, the best overall investment for most Americans has been their houses, which have kept track with inflation and appreciated an average of approximately four percent a year. Generalities and averages, however, do not apply to every situation, and past performance never offers a guarantee for future performance.

One geographical region (even a micro-region within a city) may increase dramatically in price while its neighbor remains flat. The following year could see the flat neighbor appreciate while the first region actually depreciates.

Consequently, your personal residence should not be viewed primarily as an investment, although it offers the likely benefit of appreciation over time as well as a place to live.

In spite of market fluctuations, the desirability of personal home ownership is not likely to change unless we experience another Great Depression, in which case all other investments are equally at risk. If you can't pay your real estate taxes in a bad economy, you can lose your house in three years (in most states). However, if you can't pay the mortgage payments, you can lose it in three months.

It is unfortunate that most Americans have come to accept long-term debt on their houses as normal. The high expense of housing—particularly in some markets—requires most young couples to get a 30-year mortgage to make the monthly payments affordable. However, by controlling their lifestyle and prepaying their principal a little bit each month, most families can pay off a house in 15 years or so.

EFFECTS OF PAYING MORE EACH MONTH ON A $100,000 MORTGAGE AT 9 PERCENT				
Extra amount paid	Principal/ Interest	Life of loan (years)	Interest paid	Interest saved
None	$804.62	30.00	$189,667.95	0
$25 monthly	$829.62	26.17	$160,222.62	$29,445.33
$50 monthly	$854.62	23.42	$140,227.01	$49,440.94
$100 monthly	**$904.62**	**19.75**	**$113,872.30**	**$75,795.65**

A simple investment strategy to follow is to make the ownership of your house your first investment priority. Then use the monthly mortgage payments you were making to start your savings for education or retirement.

Financial institutions are in the business of loaning money, and they have done a good job of inducing us to borrow. More than 70 percent of Americans under age 65 do not own their houses debt free.

There is no better time to start paying off your debts than right now, and it begins with an attitude adjustment. This adjustment is to make up your mind that God's Word—not someone else's idea of financial logic—governs your decisions.

Cars

Owning a car is the norm in our society. Outside of the largest urban areas where public transportation is sufficient, owning at least one car is a practical necessity. So what is the most economical way to buy one?

Examine Your Motives

Most cars are sold because of buyers' wants rather than their needs. In fact, most car shoppers are simply tired of their current car; it looks out of date or needs some repairs. In many cases, they want to keep up with their neighbors or coworkers. Sometimes they just need a mood adjustment, which a new car certainly provides—for a short time.

We have been programmed to think that if any of these conditions exist we need a new car. Certainly cars do wear out, and we will all eventually need to get another car; but we should examine our motives first to make sure we are not caving in to an emotional need rather than a transportation need. A different car can solve a transportation need, but it will only deepen the emotional need if it involves a greater debt burden.

Bottom line—buy an automobile for the right reason, and pray for His wisdom when you begin the buying process.

Determine Your Needs

Having examined your motives, the next step is to determine your needs. Who wouldn't like to drive the latest greatest? Unfortunately, may people shop with this perspective: "I'll find the car I want, and if the salesman can come up with financing that allows me to drive it off, it must be God's will." That's a disaster in the making.

Consider these questions:

1. What do I need?

2. What is the best value?

3. What does my spending plan allow (considering all ownership costs)?

4. What is the best stewardship of my family's hard-earned money?

Costs (payments, insurance, maintenance) for a mid-range new car commonly run in excess of $500 a month. That kind of expense can wreck the average family's spending plan.

Sure, they may be able to make the monthly payments, but the other categories, like Food and Clothes, will begin to suffer. Since these are major needs, the family will inevitably go into debt to get them.

The average family needs to buy a good quality, reliable used car. The size, style, age, and appearance of that car will vary from family to family. Unfortunately, many people can't overcome the temptation to buy a new car. Furthermore, a young couple who buys a new car may be starting a lifetime habit. They may become accustomed to buying every four years, which can cost an incredible amount of money, especially if these new car purchases are made on credit.

Dr. Floyd Vest, with the mathematics department at the University of North Texas, has calculated the financial impact of a family buying a new car on credit every four years beginning in 1990. The illustration family always has two cars, one of which is four years older than the other. When the older one is eight years old, they trade it for a new one.

Using constant factors for each purchase (5 percent inflation, 12 percent interest, 20 percent down payment), it proves the tremendous expense of regular new car purchases. The illustration family paid $15,000 for the first new car. Beginning with the third car, the 20 percent down payment was assumed to come entirely from the trade-in value of the eight-year-old car being replaced.

Over a 56-year period, the family spent more than $1.25 million on new cars! This is much more than the average home purchase expense. And imagine the investment that would accumulate if some of this money were put to work for you rather than against you.

Be an Informed Buyer

Doing your homework before you begin shopping for a car can help you find the car best suited to your needs.

Consumer advocacy groups and publications, such as *Consumer Reports*, track the safety, maintenance, and value of each model. And remember that cheaper does not always mean better.

Friends and family members are also a good source of information. Talk with owners of cars similar to the model you are considering to see if they are satisfied.

The Old Gas Mileage Excuse

It's very common for couples to justify buying a new car because it gets better gas mileage than their existing car. Usually, they're just tired of their existing car and need an excuse to buy a new one.

Crown has coached many people who bought new cars on the basis of mileage. Unfortunately, until they sat down with a counselor, they never figured out just how much mileage savings it would take to equal the cost of a new car. In some cases, they would have to drive their new car almost 50 years to reap mileage savings equal to the car's cost.

Shopping For a Used Car

Once you have determined the type of car you want and can afford, the next step is to find it. Go to your closest friends first. Let them know you're looking for a car. Find out if there is a family in your church with a car to sell that will fit your need.

Before most Christians will sell their cars to people they know, they will either reveal everything that is wrong with the cars or else have them fixed.

By purchasing directly from the owner, you can learn the history of the car and usually negotiate the best possible price.

Leasing Companies

A second good source of used cars is a leasing company. Many of these companies keep their cars one or two years and then resell them.

Most of these cars have been routinely maintained, have low mileage, and are sold for a fair price. Often a car obtained from a leasing company will have a one-year warranty.

Banks

Bankers are another good source of used cars. Let your banker know you are interested in a really good repossession if one comes in.

Be aware that a repossessed car may need some repairs, since its owner most likely couldn't afford to maintain it properly. Have money in reserve for this purpose.

Car Dealers

Dealers have the largest selection of used cars available. A used car that was locally owned can be a good deal if you're able to contact the previous owner to see if the car has any hidden problems.

Advertisements

The difficulty in using this source for used cars is that you don't know the seller, and the seller doesn't know you. Unfortunately, there are a lot of unethical people with cars for sale.

Before buying any used car, it is advisable to write an affidavit saying, "I swear that the car I am selling, to my knowledge, has no obvious defects, no rust that I know about, and no false odometer reading." Have the seller sign it (before a notary if possible). Most honest people won't object, and most dishonest ones won't sign it.

Finally, have a mechanic check the car for defects or problems that may not be obvious to you, such as hidden rust, signs of having been in an accident, and engine problems. The dollars you spend having a mechanic look at the car are peanuts compared to the grief and expense you could be forced to deal with later.

Used Car Buying Tips

Before buying a used car, first determine what kind of car you want. Otherwise, you could be led in many different directions.

Perhaps the make and model you want is available as a "program car." These are lease and rental cars that have been bought back by dealers. They offer low mileage and a lower price than you'd pay for the same make and model if you bought it new.

When buying a used car, check a number of key areas for problems. Open all doors, the trunk, and the hood to see if the car has been repainted.

It may be that the vehicle was involved in a front- or rear-end collision. If you look under the hood and find the stickers are missing, that's a good sign that the car has been repainted.

When checking the engine, open the oil cap. If it's black inside and you see burnt oil on the valves, you know there's a problem. You also can pull out the dipstick to check for water in the oil. In addition, you can rev up the engine to check for valve or lifter noise or rod knocking.

Of course, steam coming out from under the hood and smoke coming out from the exhaust are signs of problems.

Brakes are another item you want to check. If the car shakes or vibrates when you brake, it may be an indication that a rotor is warped. Also check the brake pads. When the pads wear completely down, the metal portion of the brake scrapes against the rotor or drum and causes serious damage.

Also check:

- Air conditioning
    - Tires for remaining tread
        - Lights and electrical system (be sure everything works, including the radio, automatic seat belts, adjustable seats, windows, all other electronic components)

- Upholstery

- Carpet

It is best to have the car checked by a reliable mechanic.

Finally, before you visit any dealership, research your market area and find an established dealer who ranks high in customer satisfaction.

Safety Considerations

According to the Insurance Institute for Highway Safety in Arlington, Virginia, safety has become a major consideration—right along with quality—for people buying a car.

You obviously want to protect yourself and your family to the greatest extent possible. But there's a secondary reason for this concern about safety, and that reason is financial.

Consider this scenario: You're driving in the rain and you stop suddenly to avoid hitting a dog in the road. Because your vehicle is not equipped with antilock brakes, the brakes lock up and your car slides off the road. The land beside the road is relatively flat and clear, allowing the car to slow down before it finally comes to rest against a tree.

No one is hurt, but the side of the car is damaged and will need expensive repairs. If your car had been equipped with antilock brakes, you might have avoided the accident. More importantly, antilock brakes could help you avoid a more serious accident in which someone could be seriously hurt.

One other general safety consideration: Small cars are not as safe as larger ones. In relation to their numbers on the road, small cars account for about twice as many deaths as large cars.

Buying the Car

A listener to one of our radio programs once wrote,

"We're considering buying a new car. But with new car prices so high, we can't afford the payments on a three-year note. Our bank offers a six-year loan with a balloon payment after three years. My husband likes this plan because he says we'll obviously be making a lot higher salary by then. But the whole concept of this frightens me. What do you think?"

Buying cars with long-term loans is like playing economic roulette. Consider several problems with this six-year balloon note.

1. This woman's husband was presuming on the future. He was presuming that he and his wife would be making higher salaries when this balloon note comes due in three years.

2. He wanted a car that was too expensive for his family's spending plan. If he and his wife couldn't afford to save money and pay cash for the car, they shouldn't buy a car that expensive.

3. He wanted a car that he couldn't pay off before it was totally depreciated, which is another indication that the car was too expensive for his family's spending plan.

4. He wasn't in agreement with his wife about buying the car. God works

through both the husband and the wife in a marriage. They are a team. Genesis 2:24 says the husband and wife are one person. A divided mind on a financial issue is a red flag.

Get the most out of your existing car, and while you're driving it, set aside money for your next one. In most cases, it is a lot less expensive to repair your car than to replace it. When it makes more economic sense to replace it, consider a good used car.

Proverbs 10:22 says the blessing of the Lord should be the thing that makes us rich, not worldly possessions. God's blessing will add no sorrow to our lives, but when we buy things that exceed our spending plan, we lose our peace of mind. Long-term loans for a car we can't afford will add a lot of sorrow to our lives.

The best way to finance a car is not to finance it at all! It is always the best policy to save the money and pay cash for your car. Auto financing is poor stewardship. If, in spite of this counsel, you find that you must finance a car, here are some good basic guidelines.

Do Not Finance Through the Car Dealership

Arrange a loan through a bank or other financial institution ahead of time so you can negotiate with the dealer on a cash basis. Be sure it is a simple interest loan with no pay-off restrictions. If you do that, at least you have the capability to become debt free in a short period of time.

Do Not Trade in Your Old Car; Sell It Instead

If a car dealer can sell your car and make a profit, so can you. It takes more time and effort to sell your car, but the effort is worthwhile. Advertise in the newspaper and online and put a sign in the car window. If your car is in reasonable shape, it shouldn't take very long to sell.

The main goal when purchasing an automobile is to educate yourself, pray for wisdom, expect God to meet your needs, and enjoy the experience of knowing that God wants His best for you.

 Questions And Answers

Should I Buy an Extended Warranty on My New Car?

If you are considering an extended warranty, ask questions.

1. Does the warranty cover a period of time or a number of miles not covered under any implied warranties?

2. Does the extended warranty cover parts and labor, or parts only?

3. Does the price of the warranty seem reasonable in relation to the price of the parts covered?

    If an extended warranty covers 5 years/50,000 miles, then the coverage will probably last less than five years because the average person drives more than 10,000 miles per year. A better warranty would cover 5 years/100,000 miles.

If only parts are covered, the cost of labor is usually so great that the owner won't get the full benefit of buying the extended warranty unless each part covered is more expensive than the relative cost of the warranty.

How Much of Our Family Budget Should Be Designated for Car Expenses?

About 13 percent of your Net Spendable Income (income after deducting tithe and taxes) should be allotted for car expenses. These expenses include payments, gas, oil, maintenance, insurance, and some savings for a future replacement of the vehicle.

What Are Some Ways I Can Cut My Car Expenses?

1. Look for savings on car insurance. If your car is more than five years old, you may want to consider only liability coverage, which is required by law. Or you might choose a policy with a higher deductible. Shop and compare prices.

2. Save money on tires. Go to a tire dealer and ask if he sells "take-offs," which are tires that have been taken off a new car because the buyer wanted a different kind. Take-offs are nearly new and may be half the price.

3. Consider starting a car maintenance co-op or join an existing one. A typical co-op involves a group of Christians who meet regularly at a church parking lot to perform routine maintenance and car repairs for one another.

Preventive maintenance will save on towing charges due to unexpected breakdowns on the highway. Check your local library for books on car ownership that offer other money-saving tips.

What About Leasing a Car?

Leasing seems attractive to those who cannot otherwise afford a new car. But as the old saying goes, there is no free lunch.

The average new car is over $20,000, and as soon as you drive it off the lot you have a used car with a new car loan on it.

Loans involve down payments, and some people don't have enough savings to meet even this requirement. Since leasing involves little or no down payment, it is a convenient way to get a new car. But that convenience comes at a high price because there is more involved than just monthly payments.

It definitely costs more to lease a car than to purchase one over the same period of time because of the higher processing expense of a complex lease agreement and the added profit layer of the lease itself. Although leasing companies have the advantage of buying cars at a volume discount, the discount isn't much greater than an astute buyer can get on his own.

At the end of a lease period, you still owe a percentage of the car's value if you want to buy it. So you don't avoid the costs. You just string them out over a longer period of time. And then there are the potential penalties at the end of the lease:

1. If you drive too many miles (usually more than 10,000 per year), you'll

pay a steep penalty for each excess mile.

2. If the car has "excessive" wear, you could pay another 10 percent. And if the car is generally downgraded, you could be required to pay an additional 10 percent.

You can watch the mileage during the lease term to gauge your excess mileage penalties, but the other potential penalties are more subjective, leaving you in jeopardy until you return the car.

In general, leasing is a better value when the costs can be deducted as a business expense, but most families cannot do this.

Bouncing Back:
Charlie and Julia Sizemore

Although saving for future purchases was once a way of life, it has become a lost art in today's credit culture. Charlie and Julia Sizemore, whose family is well on its way to getting out of debt after years of relying on credit cards, have rediscovered its value.

"I've got an engineering degree and a master's in business," Charlie said. "For years I've been in control of and responsible for multimillion-dollar operations, and I could do it well. I could nail a million-dollar budget within 2 percent, but I could not get within 15 percent of a home budget."

Charlie's 20-plus-year career as a petroleum engineer has been a rocky road for him, his wife Julia, and their two teen-age daughters, Lindsay and Kristen.

He entered Texas Tech University during the Texas oil boom of the 1970s, when significant financial benefits were assured to recent petroleum engineering grads.

Three years later, right before he graduated, the oil boom had become an oil bust, and Charlie's career since has been marked by multiple layoffs, withdrawals from the Texas Employment Commission, long-distance commuting, and relocating.

Julia nodded with a smile. "The wives have a joke. It's not 'Has your husband been laid off?' but 'How many times has your husband been laid off?'"

Like many of his coworkers, Charlie and his family weathered the bad times by depending on credit cards.

"When the oil industry was down, we used our credit cards quite a bit; we didn't even think about it. We just kept using them and using them and realized we had incurred a tremendous amount of debt," Charlie said.

The family's attitudes toward money would change as drastically as their surroundings when Charlie's latest job change took them across the state of Texas, from the small city of Midland to the outskirts of Dallas.

Julia recalled the billboard that introduced them to Crown Financial Ministries.

"We were driving down Loop-820 and saw on the billboard of Richland Hills

Church, 'Want to find out what God has to say about your money?'"

When she and Charlie attended the church service that Sunday, Julia pointed to the Crown announcement in the bulletin and told her husband, "This is why we're here."

One Crown life group and two years later, the Sizemores have reduced their debt by 30 percent; Julia is running her own Web design business; and the whole family has benefited from a shared responsibility in their finances.

"It's opened up a lot of lines of communication because all four of us are more aware of where we are financially," Julia said. "Now we all sit down, and if there's a need, we look at the need; or if there's something that we want, we start saving for that."

The Sizemores saw more stability in their lives when they gave God a bigger role in their career and personal financial decisions.

Living by God's provision has alleviated many sleepless nights for Charlie, who had always worried about the future. He'd like to help others find that same sense of peace about their finances. He's eager to help people cope with financial stress because he knows what debt and unemployment feel like. Charlie now serves as a Crown Money Map Coach Trainer.

"I primarily want to work with young couples to keep them from making the mistakes I made," Charlie said. "It never would have occurred to me, 22 years old with a college degree, that I needed to look to the Bible for financial advice."

For Charlie's family, changing bad spending habits did not come easily; it took both commitment and the grace of God.

"If we had not had Crown, we'd still be ignoring [our debt]," he said. "It took us 10 years to get there, and we've been working on it solid for three years now. . . . I think the first six months you're just changing habits. It's kind of like putting the brakes on and then you start moving backward."

Julia said they plan to be credit card free in three years and completely debt-free in 10 years. As they make steady progress, they are encouraged by God's blessings.

"If you're faithful with what you're doing, God takes care of you," Julia said. "Periodically, God sends us little checks. . . . We'll get a refund [that] matches exactly where we need to be in our budget."

Like her husband, Julia wants to share her wisdom with others. She serves on the Dallas/Fort Worth Crown City Team and has led the Crown Teen Study. Having applied the principles she learned in Crown to her own Web design business, Julia is leading a group of business women through Larry Burkett's study, *Business by the Book*. She is starting her company slowly, without accumulating debt, and donating her services to ministries.

In addition to finding more ways to serve, the Sizemores also have experienced the joy of giving. "Even though we are still on a very strict budget, we've been able to give more money than we've ever been able to give, and I've really enjoyed that," Julia said.

Charlie and Julia have already begun instructing their daughters in godly stewardship. For example, they required Lindsay and Kristen to participate in a Crown life group study before opening checking accounts, and they expect their daughters to print out budgets and balance checkbooks. Julia does not want her children to learn financial discipline the hard way.

"We've been through some very interesting times," she said. "But when you put it all in perspective, and you turn to God, you know that it's all okay. When you look back, God knew exactly what He was doing." ■

Your Response

Action Steps _____

_____

_____

_____

_____

_____

_____

_____

_____

_____

_____

Celebration Plan _____

_____

_____

_____

_____

_____

_____

_____

CHAPTER 3

WRAPPING IT UP WITH HOPE

So, would you like your spending plan to balance and to cover your needs? And would you like to buy a house or a car or some other major purchase in a prudent way—a way that allows you to rest comfortably without high-risk indebtedness? Good! You have more going for you than you might think.

There is much more to these equations than simple money math. That's just the surface. Beneath the surface is where you find true treasure. Beneath the surface is the heart of your greatest benefactor.

Don't make the mistake of thinking that this brief chapter is theological theory or that it doesn't speak to your needs in a practical way. This is as practical as it gets, because it deals with getting in the flow of God's will. No economic plan—including the perfect spending plan—can accomplish what you need the most.

What do you _really_ believe?

Do you believe God has more interest in your welfare than you do? As self-centered as we naturally are, it's hard to believe, isn't it? But it's the theme of His message to us throughout the entire Bible.

God's Spirit constantly strives to cut through our fallen perspective and give us a more accurate view of reality. He wants us to know that He's not holding out on us; He's holding out for us. Even the Ten Commandments were not given to us for His benefit; they were given to protect us!

Are you aware that God is watching over you with unfailing love and care? Consider this: *"…Your Father knows what you need before you ask Him"* (Matthew 6:8).

It's a simple sentence, easy to glide over without reflecting on its importance to your personal situation. But gliding over what Jesus says is always a mistake. Think through it for a moment.

1. **The speaker, Jesus, is the creator of the universe.** *"Through him all things were made; without him nothing was made that has been made"* (John 1:3, NIV). His understanding and power are unlimited, His authority and credibility beyond question. If He had been a mere man, His statement would be as meaningful as the words of any prophet, but He was not a mere man. Reflect for a moment on the credentials of the one making the statement.

2. **The speaker, Jesus, knows the Father intimately.** His knowledge does not rely on the descriptions and testimonies of others; it is not a faith-based acceptance of something unseen and yet hoped for. He and the Father are one. *"No one has*

*ever seen God, but God the One
and Only, who is at the Father's
side, has made him known"* (John
1:18, NIV).

3. **Jesus identifies the Father as "your
   Father."** He is not distant and uninvolved.
   Think of the most loving, perfect earthly father
   you can imagine—all he would do for the welfare of his
   children—and realize that he is merely a dim reflection
   of "your Father." God spared nothing, including His
   only Son, for you. Can you trust "your Father"?

4. **"Your Father knows what you need."** How could
   it be otherwise? Our inability to see Him causes us to
   doubt whether He is really there. Our inability to always
   get our way—to get instant gratification of our every
   prayer—causes us to wonder whether prayer really
   works, whether He is really listening, whether He really
   gets it. Jesus assures us that the Father gets it.

5. **"Before you ask Him."** Notice that Jesus never says
   we shouldn't ask. He doesn't conclude that our asking
   is unnecessary; He merely emphasizes the point that
   the Father is so aware of our needs that He doesn't
   have to rely on us to inform Him. Our asking is an exercise for our benefit rather than for His education.

It's all about trust.

God uses money as an ongoing laboratory in our lives to
increase our trust in Him—Whom we cannot see—over
everything else, including money, which we can see—very
clearly. Until we get to the place where we trust more in God's

good provision than in our temporal treasures, He has to keep repeating the experiments—sometimes painful—designed to open our eyes to His perspective.

Let your heart hear what Jesus pleads with His audience to see—not just in the abstract—but in the reality of their daily lives.

> *"Therefore I tell you, do not worry about your life, what you will eat or drink; or about your body, what you will wear. Is not life more important than food, and the body more important than clothes? Look at the birds of the air; they do not sow or reap or store away in barns, and yet your heavenly Father feeds them. Are you not much more valuable than they? Who of you by worrying can add a single hour to his life?*
>
> *"And why do you worry about clothes? See how the lilies of the field grow. They do not labor or spin. Yet I tell you that not even Solomon in all his splendor was dressed like one of these. If that is how God clothes the grass of the field, which is here today and tomorrow is thrown into the fire, will he not much more clothe you, O you of little faith?"* (Matthew 6:25-30, NIV).

We don't want to be people of "little faith," but we are naturally attuned to the limitations of our five senses. Unfortunately, our senses can never perceive the extent of God's reality even though creation reflects His splendor. Jesus continues his message with a clear implication: "Don't you get it? You can trust your Father to supply!"

"So do not worry, saying, 'What shall we eat?' or 'What shall we drink?' or 'What shall we wear?' For the pagans run after all these things, and your heavenly Father knows that you need them. But seek first his kingdom and his righteousness, and all these things will be given to you as well. Therefore do not worry about tomorrow, for tomorrow will worry about itself. Each day has enough trouble of its own" (Matthew 6:31-34, NIV).

True faith puts first things first.

Do you see the key? Verse 33 gives us God's perspective on life's equation. It's all about putting first things first. To put it in its classic propositional form, God is saying, "Look, I know this takes faith, but if you put Me first, I will take care of you. Period. And putting Me first means trusting Me, so stop worrying about what you can't control."

Putting God first means diligently following His direction to the best of our ability. We don't sit idly by, expecting Him to pull rabbits out of the hat and hand them to us. We act in accordance with His instructions. We work. We give. We save. We deal honestly. We repay our debts. We live the law of love. But then, having done our best to handle money—and every other part of our life—according to His direction, we rest in perfect confidence that He will provide for our needs and that He will never leave or forsake us. We plan, but we don't worry.

Jesus continues His message by driving the point:

"Ask and it will be given to you; seek and you will find; knock and the door will be opened to you. For everyone who asks receives; he who seeks finds; and to him who knocks, the door will be opened.

"Which of you, if his son asks for bread, will give him a stone? Or if he asks for a fish, will give him a snake? If you, then, though you are evil, know how to give good gifts to your children, how much more will your Father in heaven give good gifts to those who ask him!" (Matthew 7:7-11, NIV).

This is not a new message. Jesus was just delivering it in a new way and demonstrating it in His sacrificial life. It's an extension of a hope-filled directive from the Old Testament.

"Trust in the LORD and do good; dwell in the land and enjoy safe pasture. Delight yourself in the LORD and he will give you the desires of your heart. Commit your way to the LORD; trust in him and he will do this" (Psalm 37:3-5, NIV).

If you want the desires of your heart—and who doesn't?— both the Old and New Testaments give us the same formula. "Trust…do good…delight…commit…trust."

Do a self-check.

How do you know if you're trusting? Jesus offers a simple test. *"So in everything, do to others what you would have them do to you, for this sums up the Law and the Prophets"* (Matthew 7:12, NIV).

You can't live the Golden Rule without trust, because sometimes you will suffer for it. It requires you to act independently of what you receive from others. You can't do that without believing that somehow God will deal with the injustices you will suffer.

Do you treat people as well as they deserve? If so, you fail the test. That's the standard by which the world lives. Jesus calls us to a radical standard, one that operates in dramatic contrast to the world's. Instead of merely treating people as *we* think they deserve—setting ourselves as their judge—we are to treat them as we *want* to be treated.

When you honestly follow the Golden Rule, your actions demonstrate your trust; when you do not, they betray any hollow declaration of trust in God.

Start fresh, with new hope.

Make it your goal to grow daily in faith, trusting God with everything that is dear to you. Trust and obey. Ask, seek, knock. Make your wishes known, committing your way to Him.

As you create and implement your spending plan and save for big-ticket purchases, remember to put first things first. God—not your employer, lender or retirement plan—is your Provider. "…Your Father knows what you need before you ask him."

> "What, then, shall we say in response to this? If God is for us, who can be against us? He who did not spare his own Son, but gave him up for us all—how will he not also, along with him, graciously give us all things?" (Romans 8:31-32, NIV).

Your Response

Action Steps

_____

_____

_____

_____

_____

_____

_____

_____

_____

Celebration Plan

_____

_____

_____

_____

_____

_____

_____

INTRODUCTION TO CHRIST

As important as our financial welfare is, it is not our highest priority. The single most important need of every person everywhere is to know God and experience the gift of His forgiveness and peace.

These five biblical truths will show you God's open door through a personal relationship with Jesus Christ.

1. God loves you and wants you to know Him and experience a meaningful life.

God created people in His own image, and He desires a close relationship with each of us. *"For God so loved the world, that He gave His only begotten Son, that whoever believes in Him shall not perish, but have eternal life"* (John 3:16). *"I [Jesus] came that they might have life, and have it abundantly"* (John 10:10).

God the Father loved you so much that He gave His only Son, Jesus Christ, to die for you.

2. Unfortunately, we are separated from God.

Because God is holy and perfect, no sin can abide in His presence. Every person has sinned, and the consequence of sin is separation from God. *"All have sinned and fall short of the glory of God"* (Romans 3:23). *"Your sins have cut you off from God"* (Isaiah 59:2, TLB).

3. God's only provision to bridge this gap is Jesus Christ.

Jesus Christ died on the cross to pay the penalty for our sin, bridging the gap between God and us. Jesus said, *"I am the way, and the truth, and the life; no one comes to the Father but through Me"* (John 14:6). *"God demonstrates His own love towards us, in that while we were yet sinners, Christ died for us"* (Romans 5:8).

4. This relationship is a gift from God.

Our efforts can never achieve the perfection God requires. The only solution was to provide it to us as a gift.

When Jesus bore our sins on the cross, paying our penalty forever, He exchanged His righteousness for our guilt. By faith, we receive the gift we could never deserve.

Is that fair? Of course not! God's love exceeds His justice, resulting in mercy and grace toward us.

"It is by grace you have been saved, through faith— and this is not from yourselves, it is the gift of God— not by works, so that no one can boast" (Ephesians 2:8-9, NIV).

5. We must each receive Jesus Christ individually.

Someone has said that God has no grandchildren. Each of us is responsible before God for our own sin. We can continue to bear the responsibility and pay the consequences or we can receive the gift of Jesus' righteousness, enabling God to declare us "Not guilty!"

If you desire to know the Lord and are not certain whether you have this relationship, we encourage you to receive Christ right now. Pray a prayer similar to this suggested one:

> **"God, I need You. I invite Jesus to come into my life as my Savior and Lord and to make me the person You want me to be. Thank You for forgiving my sins and for giving me the gift of eternal life."**

You may be successful in avoiding financial quicksand—and we pray you will be—but without a relationship with Christ, it won't have lasting value. Eternal perspective begins with Him.

If you ask Christ into your life, please tell some people you know who are also following Christ. They will encourage you and help you get involved in a Bible-teaching church where you can grow spiritually. And please let us know as well. We would love to help in any way we can.

GOD'S OWNERSHIP & FINANCIAL FAITHFULNESS

How we view God determines how we live. Viewing Him as Savior is a good beginning, but growth comes when we view Him as Lord.

After losing his children and all his possessions, Job continued to worship God because he knew God was the Lord of those possessions and retained the ultimate rights over them. Realizing that God owed him nothing and he owed God everything enabled him to submit to God's authority and find contentment.

Moses walked away from his earthly inheritance, regarding *"disgrace for the sake of Christ as of greater value than the treasures of Egypt"* because he had his eye on God's reward (Hebrews 11:26, NIV).

Our willingness, like theirs, to give up a lesser value for a greater one, requires recognizing what most of the world does not: God is not only the Creator and Owner of all but also the ultimate definer of value. Those responsibilities belong to Him. He has retained them because He alone is capable of handling them.

Most of the frustration we experience in handling money comes when we take God's responsibilities on our own shoulders. Successful money management requires us to understand three aspects of God's Lordship—three roles for which He retains responsibility.

1. GOD OWNS IT ALL.

God owns all our possessions. *"To the Lord your God belong . . . the earth and everything in it"* (Deuteronomy 10:14, NIV). *"The earth is the Lord's, and all it contains"* (Psalm 24:1).

Leviticus 25:23 identifies Him as the owner of all the land: *"The land . . . shall not be sold permanently, for the land is Mine."* Haggai 2:8 says that He owns the precious metals: *"'The silver is Mine and the gold is Mine,' declares the Lord of hosts."*

Even our body—the one thing for which we would tend to claim total ownership—is not our own. *"Or do you not know that your body is a temple of the Holy Spirit who is in you, whom you have from God, and that you are not your own?"* (1 Corinthians 6:19).

The Lord created all things, and He never transferred the ownership of His creation to people. In Colossians 1:17 we are told that, *"In Him all things hold together."* At this very moment the Lord holds everything together by His power. As we will see throughout this study, recognizing God's ownership is crucial in allowing Jesus Christ to become the Lord of our money and possessions.

• Yielding Our Ownership to His Lordship

If we are to be genuine followers of Christ, we must transfer owner-ship of our possessions to Him. *"None of you can be My disciple who does not give up all his own possessions"* (Luke 14:33). Sometimes He tests us by asking us to give up the very possessions that are most important to us.

The most vivid example of this in Scripture is when God instructed Abraham, *"Take now your son, your only son, whom you love, Isaac . . . and offer him there as a burnt offering"* (Genesis 22:2). When Abraham obeyed, demonstrating his willingness to give up his most valuable possession, God responded, *"Do not lay a hand on the boy . . . now I know that you fear God, because you have not withheld from Me your son"* (Genesis 22:12, NIV).

When we acknowledge God's ownership, every spend-ing decision becomes a spiritual decision. No longer do we ask, "Lord, what do You want me to do with my money?" It becomes, "Lord, what do You want me to do with Your money?" When we have this attitude and handle His money according to His wishes, spending and saving decisions become as spiritual as giving decisions.

• Recognizing God's Ownership

Our culture—the media, even the law—says that what you possess, you own. Acknowledging God's ownership requires a transformation of thinking, and this can be difficult. Many people say that God owns it all while they cling desperately to possessions that they think define them.

Here are a number of practical suggestions to help us recognize God's ownership.

- For the next 30 days, meditate on 1 Chronicles 29:11-12 when you first awake and just before going to sleep.

- For the next 30 days, ask God to make you aware of His ownership and help you to be thankful for it.

- Establish the habit of acknowledging God's ownership every time you buy something.

Recognizing God's ownership is important in learning contentment. When you believe you own something, you are more vulnerable to its circumstances. If it suffers loss or damage, your attitude can swing quickly from happy to discontented.

Recognizing it as God's loss doesn't make it irrelevant, but it does change your perspective. Now you can focus on how He will use this incident in causing *"all things to work together for good to those who love God, to those who are called according to His purpose"* (Romans 8:28).

2. GOD CONTROLS IT ALL.

Besides being Creator and Owner, God is ultimately in control of every event that occurs upon the earth. *"We adore*

*you as being in control of every-
thing"* (1 Chronicles 29:11, TLB).
*"Whatever the Lord pleases, He
does, in heaven and in earth"* (Psalm
135:6). And in the book of Daniel,
King Nebuchadnezzar stated: *"I praised
the Most High; I honored and glorified him
who lives forever. . . . He does as he pleases with
the powers of heaven and the peoples of the earth. No
one can hold back his hand or say to him: 'What have
you done?'"* (Daniel 4:34-35, NIV).

God is also in control of difficult events. *"I am the Lord,
and there is no other, the One forming light and creating darkness, causing well-being and creating calamity;
I am the Lord who does all these"* (Isaiah 45:6-7).

It is important for us to realize that our heavenly Father
uses even seemingly devastating circumstances for
ultimate good in the lives of the godly. *"We know that
God causes all things to work together for good to
those who love God, to those who are called according to His purpose"* (Romans 8:28). God allows difficult
circumstances for three reasons.

• He accomplishes His intentions.

This is illustrated in the life of Joseph, who was sold
into slavery as a teenager by his jealous brothers.
Joseph later said to his brothers: *"Do not be distressed
and do not be angry with yourselves for selling me
here, because it was to save lives that God sent me
ahead of you. . . . It was not you who sent me here,
but God. . . . You intended to harm me, but God*

*intended it for good to accomplish what is now be-
ing done, the saving of many lives"* (Genesis 45:5, 8;
50:20, NIV).

• He develops our character.

Godly character, something that is precious in His
sight, is often developed during trying times. *"We also
rejoice in our sufferings, because we know that suffer-
ing produces perseverance; perseverance, character"*
(Romans 5:3-4, NIV).

• He disciplines His children.

*"Those whom the Lord loves He disciplines. . . . He
disciplines us for our good, so that we may share His
holiness. All discipline for the moment seems not to
be joyful, but sorrowful; yet to those who have been
trained by it, afterwards it yields the peaceful fruit of
righteousness"* (Hebrews 12:6,10-11).

When we are disobedient, we can expect our loving
Lord to discipline us, often through difficult circumstances. His purpose is to encourage us to abandon
our sin and to "share His holiness."

You can be at peace knowing that your loving heavenly
Father is in control of every situation you will ever face.
He will use every one of them for a good purpose.

3. GOD PROVIDES IT ALL.

God promises to provide our needs. *"Seek
first His kingdom and His righteousness,
and all these things [food and clothing]*

will be added to you" (Matthew 6:33).

The same God who fed manna to the children of Israel during their 40 years of wandering in the wilderness and who fed 5,000 with only five loaves and two fish has promised to provide our needs. This is the same God who told Elijah, *"I have commanded the ravens to provide for you there. . . . The ravens brought him bread and meat in the morning and bread and meat in the evening"* (1 Kings 17:4, 6).

God—Both Predictable and Unpredictable

God is totally predictable in His faithfulness to provide for our needs. What we cannot predict is how He will provide. He uses various and often surprising means—an increase in income or a gift. He may provide an opportunity to stretch limited resources through money-saving purchases. Regardless of how He chooses to provide for our needs, He is completely reliable.

Our culture believes that God plays no part in financial matters; they assume that His invisibility means He is uninvolved. They try to shoulder responsibilities that God never intended for them—burdens of ownership, control, and provision that only He can carry.

Jesus said, *"Come to Me, all who are weary and heavy-laden, and I will give you rest. Take My yoke upon you. . . . For My yoke is easy, and My burden is light"* (Matthew 11:28-30). This is the only way we can rest and enjoy the peace of God.

When we trust God to do His part in our finances, we can focus on doing our part: being financially faithful with every resource He has given us.

Defining Financial Faithfulness

Faithfully living by God's financial principles doesn't necessarily mean having a pile of money in the bank, but it does bring an end to overdue bills and their related stress. And that's not the most important part; that's just relief from symptoms.

Consider some of the big-picture benefits:

- Assurance that God is in control of our circumstances
- Absolute faith in His promise to meet all of our needs
- A clear conscience before God
- A clear conscience with others

This is not to say that we will live on financial autopilot with no more challenges for the rest of our lives. God promises no such thing. In fact, without challenges our faith has no opportunity to be perfected or even to grow; without challenges it isn't active or visible. But peace in the midst of challenges is a miraculous quality of life, and that's what God promises when we learn to trust and follow Him fully.

With God in control, we have nothing to fear. He is the Master of the universe. His wisdom is superior to ours in every way, and no situation is too complex or hopeless for Him to solve.

God has even provided a solution for our ongoing frailties and failings. As part of His great redemption, He offers con-

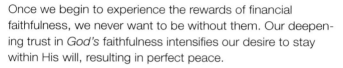

tinuing forgiveness and cleansing from all unrighteousness (1 John 1:9). We make mistakes—sometimes willfully violating His plan for us—but He welcomes our confession and honors it by restoring our fellowship and renewing our guidance.

Once we begin to experience the rewards of financial faithfulness, we never want to be without them. Our deepening trust in *God's* faithfulness intensifies our desire to stay within His will, resulting in perfect peace.

Many people have inherited or achieved financial independence: a level of wealth that requires no further work or income. But apart from Christ, they don't have freedom from anxiety; they have merely replaced one set of worries with another. They often fear:

- Loss of what they have accumulated

- Loss of meaningful relationships—fearing that others only care about what they have rather than who they are

- Loss of safety as their wealth makes them a target for theft or kidnapping

- Loss of grace from others, who jealously hold them to a higher standard because of their wealth

Being financially free, on the other hand, includes freedom from these fears as well as from the oppression of envy, covetousness, and greed.

Financial faithfulness is transformation—a process that requires God's power and our participation. It is synonymous with our definition of true financial faithfulness in the *Crown Money Map*™:

1. Knowing that God owns it all.

2. Finding contentment with what He provides.

3. Being free to be all He made you to be.

This is the big picture, the framework within which wealth and material possessions take their rightful place—not as ends but as means—in God's hands.

Steps to Cultivate Financial Faithfulness

Now it is time to outline the path. Since we're talking about transformation, you'll notice that some of our steps go well beyond mere money-management techniques.

1. TRANSFER OWNERSHIP.

Transferring ownership of every possession to God means acknowledging that He already owns them and that we will begin treating them accordingly. This includes more than just material possessions; it includes money, time, family, education, even earning potential for the future. This is essential to experience the Spirit-filled life in the area of finances (see Psalm 8:4-6).

There is no substitute for this step. If we believe we are the owners of even a single possession, then the events affecting that possession are going to affect our attitudes. God will not input His perfect will into our lives unless we first surrender our wills to Him.

However, if we make a total transfer of everything to God, He will demonstrate His ability. It is important to understand and accept God's conditions for His control (see Deuteronomy 5:32-33). God will keep His promise to provide our every need according to His perfect plan.

It is easy to say we will make a total transfer of everything to God, but it's not so easy to do. Our desire for control and our habit of self-management cause difficulty in consistently seeking God's will in the area of material things. But without a deep conviction that He is in control, we can never experience true financial faithfulness.

What a great relief it is to turn our burdens over to Him. Then, if something happens to the car, we can say, "Father, I gave this car to You; I've maintained it to the best of my ability, but I don't own it. It belongs to You, so do with it whatever You like." Then look for the blessing God has in store as a result of this attitude.

2. BECOME DEBT FREE.

God wants us to be free to serve Him without restriction. *"You were bought with a price; do not become slaves of men"* (1 Corinthians 7:23). *"The rich rules over the poor, and the borrower becomes the lender's slave"* (Proverbs 22:7).

Read *Debt and Bankruptcy*, another book in the *MoneyLife™ Basics Series*, for further information on this, including definitions and steps for getting out of debt. For most, this will involve sacrifice—at least initially—but the payoff is well worth it.

3. GIVE REGULARLY AND GENEROUSLY.

Every follower of Christ should establish tithing (10 percent of income) as a beginning point of giving and as a testimony to God's ownership. We can't say we have given total ownership to God if our actions don't back the claim.

It is through sharing that we bring His power in finances into focus. In every case, God wants us to give the first part to Him, but He also wants us to pay our creditors. This requires establishing a plan, and it will probably mean making sacrifices of wants and desires until all obligations are current.

We cannot sacrifice God's part—that is not our prerogative as faithful, obedient followers of Christ. Malachi 3:8-9 has strong words for those who "rob God." But then verses 10-12 describe His great blessing for those who tithe fully.

God, as the first giver, wants us to be like Him, and His economy rewards our generosity. *"Now this I say, he who sows sparingly will also reap sparingly, and he who sows bountifully will also reap bountifully"* (2 Corinthians 9:6).

Steps two and three combine to form an important conclusion. If, while en route to financial faithfulness, sacrifice becomes

necessary—and it almost always does—our sacrifice must not come from God's or our creditor's share. We must choose areas within our other discretionary expenses to sacrifice. Consider it an opportunity to exercise faith in God's reward for our obedience.

4. ACCEPT GOD'S PROVISION.

To obtain financial peace, recognize and accept that God's provision is used to direct each of our lives. Often Christians lose sight of the fact that God's will can be accomplished through a withholding of funds; we think that He can direct us only by an abundance of money. But God does not choose for everyone to live in great abundance. This does not imply poverty, but it may mean that God wants us to be more responsive to His day-by-day control.

Followers of Christ must learn to live on what God provides and not give in to a driving desire for wealth or the pressure brought on by comparison with others. This necessitates planning our lifestyle within the provision God has supplied. When we are content to do this, God will always help us find a way.

5. KEEP A CLEAR CONSCIENCE.

Living with integrity means dealing with the past as well as the present. Part of becoming financially faithful requires gaining a clear conscience regarding past business practices and personal dealings. Sometimes, in addition to a changed attitude, our transformation means making restitution for situations where we have wronged someone.

Tim's story is a good example. Before he accepted Christ, he cheated someone out of some money. God convicted him about this and indicated that he should go and make restitution. He contacted the person, confessed what had been done, and offered to make it right. The person refused to forgive and also refused to take any money.

Tim's ego and pride were hurt until he realized that he had been both obedient and successful. His confession was not primarily for the offended person but for his own relationship with God. He had done exactly what God had asked, and God had forgiven him. Nothing further was required.

6. PUT OTHERS FIRST.

This does not imply being a door mat; it simply means that we shouldn't profit at the unfair expense of someone else. As is often the case, attitude is all-important.

7. MANAGE TIME PRIORITIES.

A workaholic might gain wealth at the expense of the family's relational needs, but wealth alone is no indicator of financial faithfulness. And wealth gained with wrong priorities is likely to vanish. *"Do not weary yourself to gain wealth, cease from your consideration of it. When you set your eyes on it, it is* gone. *For wealth certainly makes itself wings like an eagle that flies toward the heavens"* (Proverbs 23:4-5). Even if it doesn't vanish, it can't deliver the satisfaction it promises. Don't be deceived by overcommitment to business or the pursuit of wealth.

God's priorities for us are very clear.

Priority number one is to develop our relationship with Jesus Christ.

Priority number two is our family. This includes teaching them God's Word. And that requires quality time, something that can't exist without a sufficient quantity from which to flow.

Develop the habit of a regular time to study God's Word for yourself as well as a family time that acknowledges your commitment to each other and to God.

Turn off the television, have the children do their homework early, and begin to study the Bible together. Pray for each other and for those in need. Help your children become intercessors who can pray for others and expect God to answer.

Priority number three is your work, which God intends to be an opportunity for ministry and personal development in addition to providing an income.

Priority number four is church activities and other ministry. This does not imply that it is unimportant or can be neglected, but it keeps us from using church as an excuse to let higher priorities slide. If we observe priority number one, we will not neglect our church.

8. AVOID OVER-INDULGENCE.

Jesus said, *"If anyone wishes to come after Me, he must deny himself, and take up his cross daily and follow Me"* (Luke 9:23). Once again, this is about priorities. Who wins the contest between God's claim on your life and your own pursuit of pleasure?

In Philippians 3:18-19, Paul says that many live as the enemies of the cross of Christ, and he describes them by saying, *"Their destiny is destruction, their god is their stomach, and their glory is in their shame"* (NIV).

That sounds alarmingly like much of our culture, and it takes great effort to avoid being swept along with the current.

9. GET CHRISTIAN COUNSEL.

"Without consultation, plans are frustrated, but with many counselors they succeed" (Proverbs 15:22). God admonishes us to seek counsel and not to rely solely on our own resources. People are often frustrated in financial planning because they lack the necessary knowledge. A common but tragic response is to give up. Within the body of Christ, God has supplied those who have the ability to help in the area of finances. Seek Christian counselors.

To read more on what God says about handling money, go to Crown.org and click "Bible Tools."

CROWN FINANCIAL MINISTRIES

Crown Financial Ministries® is an interdenominational Christian organization dedicated to equipping people around the world to learn, apply and teach biblical financial principles. Since 1976, Crown has taught or equipped more than 50 million people with the life-transforming message of faithfully living by God's financial principles in every area of their lives.

Through the generosity of donors and volunteers around the globe, Crown serves the followers of Christ worldwide, ranging from those entrusted with wealth to those living in desperate poverty. Regardless of their economic status, we rejoice with believers who develop a more intimate relationship with Jesus Christ, become free to serve Him, and more generously fund the Great Commission.

> ***For volunteer, short-term missions, or giving opportunities with Crown, visit us online at Crown.org or call 1-800-722-1976.***

Crown's mission is to provide you with help, hope, and insight as you seek to grow in financial faithfulness.

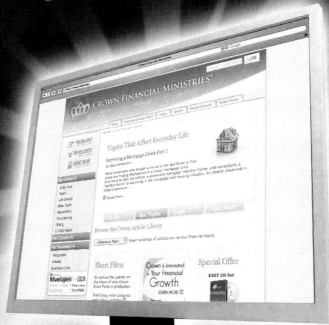

Stay Connected at Crown.org

With a comprehensive collection of online tools and resources, Crown.org will teach you how to make money, manage money, and ultimately fulfill God's purposes for your life.

God's wisdom will make a difference in your finances!

Resources

To Help You in Life and Money

Career Direct®

You have unlimited potential to be more, do more, and maximize your God-given talents and abilities. You are ready to exceed everyone's expectations.

Go to CareerDirectOnline.org to get started.

Crown Budgeting Solutions

Choose the Budgeting Solution That Fits Your Lifestyle

Paper

• Traditional option using paper, pen, and cash.

Software

• Computer software option for your PC or Mac.

Online and Mobile

• Web and Mobile option available anytime, anywhere.